HABITATS AND ENVIRONMENTS

MORE SCIENCE IN ACTION

The Marshall Cavendish Guide to Projects and Experiments

HABITATS AND ENVIRONMENTS

Compiled and created by Laura Buller and Ron Taylor

Illustrations by John Hutchinson and Stan North

Marshall Cavendish Corporation · New York · London · Toronto · Sydney

EDITORIAL STAFF

Series Editor	Laura Buller
Assistant Editors	Theresa Donaghey
	Caroline Macy
Art Editor	Keith Vollans

Production Controller	Deborah Cracknell
Production Secretary	Jayne Hough
Managing Editor	Sue Lyon
Publishing Director	Reg Wright

Reference Edition published 1990

Published by Marshall Cavendish
Corporation
147 West Merrick Road
Freeport, Long Island
N.Y. 11520

Typeset by Quadraset Ltd.
Printed in Spain

**Library of Congress Cataloging-in-
Publication Data**

Habitats and environments.
    p.   cm. — (More science in action)
  Includes index.
  Summary: Presents projects and
experiments exploring scientific principles
in different habitats and environments,
including a forest and pond.
  ISBN 1-85435-309-8
  1. Habitat (Ecology)—Experiments—
Juvenile literature. [1. Animals—Habitat—
Experiments. 2. Ecology—Experiments.
3. Experiments.] I. Marshall Cavendish
Corporation. II. Series.
QH541.24.H33   1990
574.5—dc20   90-2057
ISBN 1-85435-307-1 (set)   CIP
ISBN 1-85435-309-8 (vol)   AC

CONTENTS

Projects marked ⊹ need adult supervision.

INTRODUCTION

This book will help you learn more about science and technology. It includes experiments, projects, puzzles, and even some tricks. Some of the experiments and projects are very easy. Others are a little harder (they are marked ⊹) and you will need help from one of your teachers or parents. You do not have to begin on page 8 — look through the book and start with something you like — but remember that good scientists

- make a record of their work
- have a clean and tidy laboratory
- most important, keep themselves safe (always read pages 40 to 42 before you begin).

EASY PROJECTS

All living things — plants, animals, and people — depend on each other in some way. The branch of science concerned with the relationships living things have with each other and with their environment is called ecology. The study of habitats and environments helps us better to understand the world and all its living creatures. You can try the simple projects in the next pages to learn more. Make a butterfly farm, study seed growth and grow your own forest trees, and find out about the greenhouse effect.

Wormery

You will need—

glass jar
soil
sand
garden spade
2 or 3 earthworms
leaves
cheesecloth
rubber band
black construction
  paper
cellophane tape

Earthworms, also called nightcrawlers, move through the earth by lengthening the fronts of their segmented bodies, then contracting the backs. They live underground where we cannot see them, but if you make this wormery, you can observe the way earthworms crawl.

Procedure
1. Find a large, empty **glass jar**. You will not need a lid. Make sure that the jar is clean and dry.
2. Put a layer of damp **soil** into the jar. Then add a layer of clean **sand**. Fill the rest of the jar with more damp soil.
3. In your backyard or a nearby field, dig up a patch of earth with a **garden spade**. See if you can find two or three **earthworms**. It is easiest to find earthworms in damp, warm soil, so you might want to look for them the day after a heavy rain. Collect a few **leaves**, too.
4. Put the worms and leaves you have collected on top of the soil. Stretch a piece of **cheesecloth** over the top of the jar and hold it in place with a **rubber band**.
5. Wrap a large piece of **black construction paper** around the jar as shown. Fix the seam firmly with **cellophane tape**. Leave the jar in a safe place.
6. After a few days, take the black paper off. The burrowing worms will have dug tunnels through the soil and sand, mingling the layers.

Greenhouse effect

A thin layer of gases, including carbon dioxide and ozone, surrounds the earth. Infrared rays from the sun pass through the atmosphere easily, but some heat is reflected back to earth by carbon dioxide and certain other gases; these gases act like the glass in a greenhouse. Since the Industrial Revolution, the amount of carbon dioxide in the atmosphere has been increasing steadily, making it much more difficult for heat to escape. Global warming called the greenhouse effect may be a consequence. Try this project to observe the greenhouse effect.

Procedure

1. If you live in a warm part of the country, you can begin this experiment at any time of the year. If you live in an area that has cold winters, it is best to begin in the spring. Put some moist **soil** in two **seed trays** and plant several kinds of **flower seeds**.

2. Place a **thermometer** in each tray as shown. Cover one tray completely with **plastic wrap**. You might want to put a large **rubber band** around the second tray to secure the plastic wrap.

3. Place the trays outside, in a location which is sheltered from rain, but exposed to the sun.

4. Every week at around the same time of day, note the temperature difference between the two trays. Keep a record of your findings in a **notebook**. When the seedlings begin to grow tall, insert sticks into the sides of the plastic-wrapped tray as shown, replacing the plastic wrap carefully. You can use clean **ice cream sticks** or **wooden skewers**. Continue to note the differences between the trays. You will find that the plastic-wrapped tray is much warmer than the other tray.

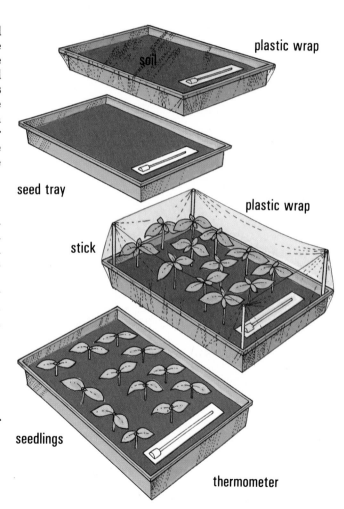

soil

plastic wrap

seed tray

plastic wrap

stick

seedlings

thermometer

You will need—

soil
2 seed trays
flower seeds
2 thermometers
plastic wrap
rubber band
notebook and pencil
ice cream sticks or
   wooden skewers

Butterfly farm

You will need—

round, shallow tin
awl or hammer and nail
string
tape measure or ruler
clear, stiff plastic or
    acetate
scissors
strong glue
old pair of pantyhose
soil
small glass jar
caterpillar
leaves

The butterfly is one of the most beautiful and fascinating of all insects. There are over 15,000 different species (kinds) of butterfly found all over the world. Their habitats range from tropical rain forests to deserts to fields and prairies.

Butterflies belong to the same insect group as moths and are often difficult to distinguish from one another. Scientists know several ways, however, to tell which insect is which. The antennae, or feelers, of a butterfly are thin with bumps at the ends, while moths have feathery antennae. The butterfly flies in the daytime, and the moth usually flies at night. When resting, the butterfly folds its wings up like the sail of a boat. A moth spreads its wings when resting like those of an airplane.

The life cycle of a butterfly has four stages. The egg stage can last anytime from a few days to months. Some eggs are invisible to the human eye, but others can be up to 1/10 of an inch in diameter. Eggs are usually laid on green plants, which will provide food for the next life stage, the larval stage. A larva, or caterpillar, emerges from the egg and immediately begins to eat. During the next two weeks or so, the larva grows rapidly. The caterpillar may molt, or shed its skin, several times during this stage to accommodate its growing body. When it reaches its full size, the larva finds a sheltered place to rest, then forms a shell called a chrysalis from silky liquid released from a tiny spinneret. During its pupa stage, the larva's structure will re-form inside the chrysalis to that of a butterfly. Anytime from a few days to a year later, the adult butterfly emerges from the chrysalis. You can observe the life cycle of a butterfly in this project.

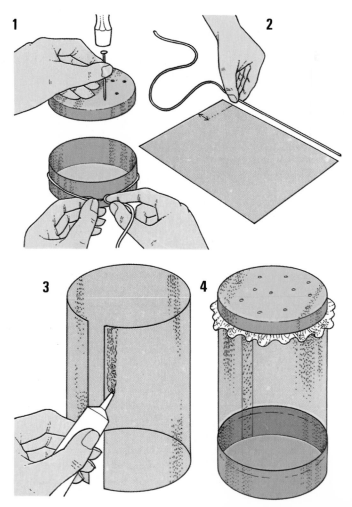

Procedure

1. Begin this project in the fall; by late December, your butterfly will be ready to emerge. You will need a **round, shallow tin** with a lid for this project. Ask an adult to punch some holes in the lid with an **awl** or a **hammer and nail**.

2. Wrap a piece of **string** around the edge of the tin lid. Then measure the string against a **tape measure** or **ruler** to find the circumference of the lid.

3. Using **scissors**, cut a piece of **clear, stiff plastic** or acetate (you can find both at an art supply store) 20 inches long and an inch wider than the circumference of the lid.

4. Use **strong glue** to join the edges of the plastic, over-lapping them as shown so that the plastic cylinder will just fit into the base of the tin. Cut a piece of nylon from an **old pair of pantyhose** to fit over the top.

5. Put a layer of **soil** into the base of the tin. Find a **small, clean jar.** Fill it with water and place it in the soil. Your cage is now ready.

6. Look around your backyard or a nearby park for a **caterpillar.** Caterpillars feed on green plants, so you might want to look for chewed leaves as a clue. Remember that most butterfly caterpillars have smooth, slender bodies, and most moth caterpillars have plump, furry bodies. Take some **leaves** along for the caterpillar to eat. Choose the type you found the caterpillar near.

7. Put the leaves in the jar of water to keep them fresh. Put the caterpillar on the leaves. Carefully put the piece of nylon and the lid on top of the cylinder. Put in fresh food when the caterpillar has eaten the leaves. Observe the life stages carefully; when your butterfly finally emerges, set it free.

Take care!

Make sure that you ask an adult to punch the air holes into the lid, and avoid touching the underside of the lid after the holes are punched.

Vegetable tops

You will need—

large carrot
knife
cotton
saucer
vegetable parer
wooden toothpick
cotton thread

You can grow a carrot top upside down—and in mid-air. Follow the directions carefully to make a miniature hanging garden from the top of a carrot.

If you wish, you can grow another plant in the "bowl" of the carrot. Follow the steps below. When your hanging garden is finished, fill the "bowl" of the carrot with moist potting soil. Then add a small plant or even a seed or two of a tiny plant, such as a dwarf nasturtium. Keep the soil moist at all times.

Procedure
1. Cut a two-inch section from the top of a large **carrot** with a **knife**. Leave any stalks and shoots attached.
2. Stand the cut end of the carrot on a layer of **cotton** in a **saucer** of water. Keep the cotton moist and the saucer in sunlight.
3. When the shoots have begun to sprout, remove the carrot top from the saucer of water. Carefully scoop a hollow bowl in the cut end, using the pointed end of a **vegetable parer**.
4. Poke a **wooden toothpick** through the top of the "bowl" as shown. Then tie equal lengths of **cotton thread** from each side of the toothpick.
5. Hang the carrot up on a hook in a sunny window. Continue to fill the "bowl" with water and do not let it become dry. Soon, the green shoots of the carrot will sprout from the bottom and grow upward toward the light.

Take care!

When using a sharp knife, always cut away from your body in case the knife slips.

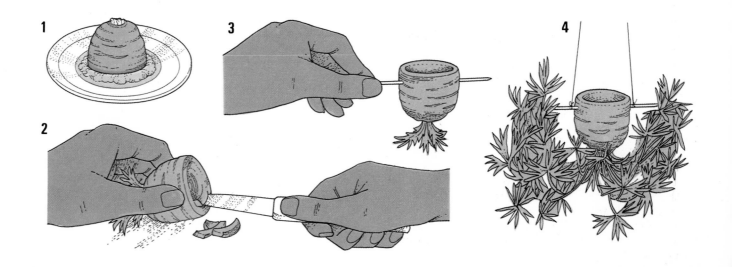

Nature museum

Have you ever thought of running your own museum? Collecting and preparing your exhibits is a fascinating pastime, and you are doubly rewarded when your family and friends come to visit it. Everything you find in fields, your backyard, nearby parks, and at the beach can be good material for a museum. When your parents or neighbors dig in their gardens, look for old bottles, pottery, and coins. If you live near a farm, try looking in freshly-plowed fields. You could find fossils in rocks near a beach. If you live near a river or creek, try combing the muddy banks for treasure. At the beach, look for driftwood, shells, pebbles, and dried strands of seaweed.

After sorting and cleaning all your finds, mount them carefully on index cards or cardboard, using glue or cellophane tape. You might want to arrange several objects on one large card as shown. Write notes on each card, describing where and when you found the exhibit and what it is.

If you find something especially interesting and want to know more about it, take it to your teacher and ask him or her to look at it. If you are lucky enough to live near a museum, take the object to the curator (the person who takes care of the museum) to look at. You might have found something rare!

If you find animal or bird bones, first try to identify them. Ask an adult to help you clean the bones. Then boil them in an old saucepan with plenty of water until all the flesh is removed. Soak them overnight in a quart of water mixed with one teaspoon of household bleach. Rinse well and dry the bones slowly. You can make them shiny if you like by painting them carefully with polyurethane varnish.

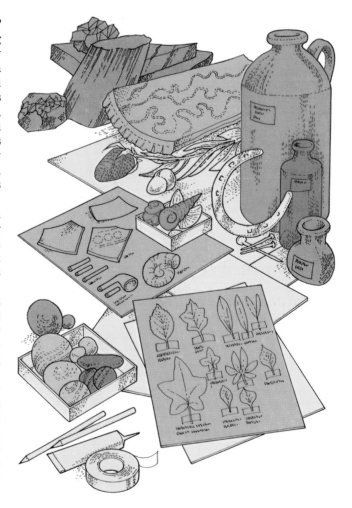

Bird feeder -⊡-

You will need—

12 inch square piece of exterior plywood
4 pieces of wooden beading, 10 inches by ½ inch
wood glue
4 nails
fine, strong cord
hammer
plastic or string netting
shelled nuts
old, heavy bowl
brush

Birds are not only beautiful and fascinating animals, they are also some of the easiest and most interesting wild creatures to observe. You can study the behavior of birds in your own backyard by building this bird feeder.

More than 700 different species of birds live in North America. Birds live in all kinds of habitats, from grasslands to seacoasts and forests, and even in urban areas. Your local bookstore or library will have an illustrated field guide which will help you to identify particular birds which live in your area.

When birdwatching, you might want to use a pair of binoculars. They will enable you to see the birds clearly without getting close enough to frighten them away.

Choose the position for your bird feeder carefully. Birds are usually attracted by trees and shrubs. They provide birds with food, like seeds and berries, and also lend shelter. Be sure to hang the bird feeder where cats cannot get to it.

During the summer months, birds can usually get all the food they need. But during the cold winter months, snow and heavy sleet make it difficult for birds to find food. You can help them by leaving food and fresh water on your bird feeder every day. Leave out a few fresh scraps, like cheese, apple cores, leftover bacon, and toast crusts. You can also buy a variety of birdseed at many grocery stores and pet shops. Birds also like shelled nuts and suet, a type of hard animal fat. Once you have attracted birds to your feeder, remember to keep feeding them. They will be used to coming to your bird feeder, and may starve if the feedings stop.

You may want to keep a record of the different birds that visit your feeder and the behavior you observe. A small notebook is ideal for making your own bird guide.

Procedure

1. You will need to ask an adult to help you build the bird feeder. Buy a **12 inch square piece of exterior plywood**, four pieces of **wooden beading** 10 inches by ½ inch, **wood glue**, **four nails**, and some **fine, strong cord**.
2. Glue the beading to the edges of the square of plywood as shown so that gaps are left at each corner. Let the glue dry completely.
3. Use a **hammer** to fix a nail into the bird feeder at all four corners, leaving the heads of the nails sticking up slightly.
4. Firmly tie a length of cord to each nail. Find a piece of old **plastic or string netting**. The kind onions or potatoes are sold in is ideal. Lay the netting out flat on a table and put some **shelled nuts** in the center. Gather the edges together to make a bag and secure firmly with strong cord. Attach one end of the cord to one of the nails in the corner of the bird feeder, if you like, so that the bag of nuts hangs freely.
5. Now wind the long lengths of cord around the branch of a tree. You might want to choose one that you can see from your bedroom window. Fill an **old, heavy bowl** with a thick rim with water and put it in the middle of the feeder. Every few days, clean the bird feeder off with a **brush**, sweeping debris out at the corners.

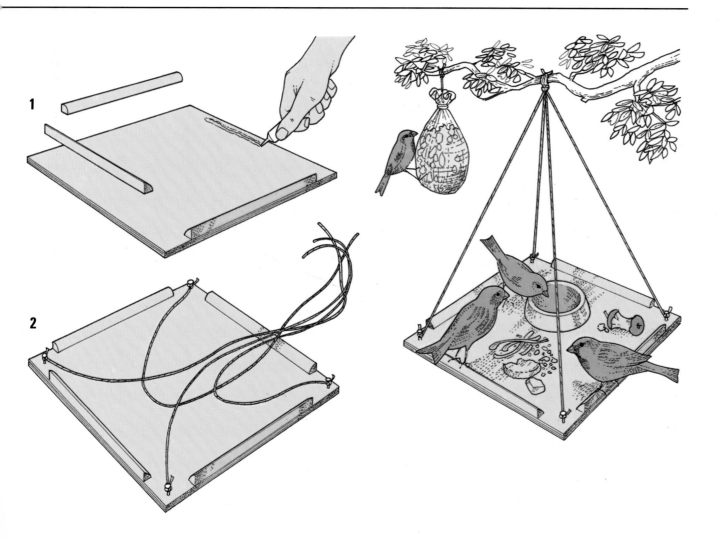

1

2

Forest trees

You will need—

ash, elm, oak, and
   maple seeds
bowl of water
4 small flowerpots
soil
shovel
wire cylinder

Growing your own forest trees from seeds is a time-consuming, but very rewarding project.

Procedure
1. In your backyard or a nearby park or woods, collect **seeds** from a variety of trees. Try to find ash, elm, oak, and maple seeds. You can use a tree guidebook or an encyclopedia to help you identify the seeds.
2. Soak the seeds in a **bowl of water** for a day or two to help loosen the seed coats.
3. After you have soaked the seeds, plant them in **small flowerpots**. Use rich garden **soil**. Different seeds take different times to germinate; in the meantime, keep the soil well watered.
4. Soon your seeds will produce saplings. Keep them in the pots, watering well, until they are several inches tall. The saplings will then be ready to plant outside. In general, early spring is the best time to plant your saplings.
5. Choose an area with fertile soil and good drainage. Remember that trees need plenty of room to grow. With a small **shovel** dig a hole large enough to hold the roots. Put the topsoil and subsoil into separate piles.
6. Carefully remove the sapling from the pot and gently stretch out the roots. Put the sapling in the hole and cover the roots with the topsoil. Fill the rest of the hole with the subsoil. Plant the other saplings in the same way. You might want to put a **wire cylinder** around the growing tree for the first year or two to protect it from animals.

ash

elm

maple

oak

Natural predators

Use a rose cutting infested with the aphid called greenfly and a ladybug to see how biological control can replace chemical pesticides.

Procedure

1. You will need a small piece of **cheesecloth**, a thick **rubber band**, a small **bottle**, and a large **glass jar** into which the bottle will easily fit. Wash both the bottle and the jar in soapy water and dry them thoroughly.

2. Find a **rose bush** that has **greenfly** on it. If you are not sure what greenfly look like, consult a gardening handbook. Use **small clippers** to cut a flower and a leafy shoot about 4 inches long with some greenfly on the leaves or stem. Place the cutting in the small bottle and add some water as shown. Then put the bottle and the cutting into the large glass jar.

3. Wherever there are greenfly, you will almost certainly find **ladybugs**. Gently take one and put it in the jar, then cover the top with the cheesecloth and secure it with the rubber band.

4. Keep watch for a few days. The ladybug is a carnivore —an animal eater—and one of its favorite foods is the aphid, or greenfly. The deliberate introduction of a predatory species of an insect like a ladybug to a crop infested with aphids is known as biological control. It is the natural alternative to using chemical pesticides that may find their way through the crop to humans. See how many greenfly the ladybug eats. After a few days, you should free the ladybug in your backyard.

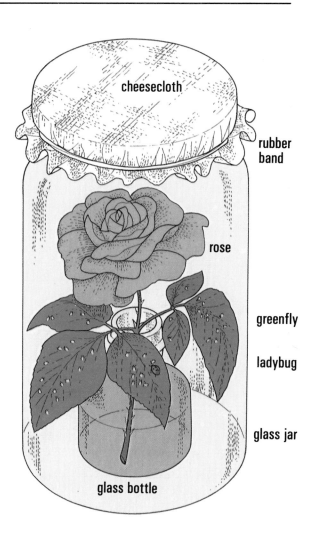

cheesecloth

rubber band

rose

greenfly

ladybug

glass jar

glass bottle

You will need—

cheesecloth
rubber band
small bottle
glass jar
rose bush, for cutting
greenfly
small clippers
ladybug

Seed growth

You will need—

corn or bean seeds
8 small dishes
blotting paper or cotton
wax pencil
baking pan
ice cubes
glass from an old
  picture frame

Do seeds grow better in warm or cold places, with or without water and air, in light or dark places? Try this experiment to find out what conditions are best for seed germination and growth.

Procedure

1. Decide upon one kind of **seed** to use for this experiment. You might want to choose corn or beans because they germinate quickly. You will be experimenting with four factors: temperature, amount of light, amount of water, and oxygen. It is important to remember that when testing one factor, the other three factors must be kept the same.

2. Find **eight small dishes**. Place a sheet of **blotting paper** or a **thin layer of cotton** in the bottom of each dish and put about a dozen of your chosen seeds on top of the paper or cotton. Using a **wax pencil**, number the plates from one to eight.

3. You will be using two dishes to test each of the four factors, one dish to experiment on and the other to serve as the control. Water dish 1; do not water dish 2. Put dish 3 in a **baking pan** or bowl filled with **ice cubes**; put dish 4 in a warm place. Put dish 5 in a dark cupboard; put dish 6 on a sunny window sill. Leave dish 7 open to the air; place a piece of **glass** from an old picture frame over dish 8.

4. After a few days, check each of the eight dishes. What happened to each pair? What conclusions can you draw about seed growth? The results of this experiment should show you that seeds need adequate water, warm temperatures, plenty of sunlight, and oxygen in order to germinate and grow.

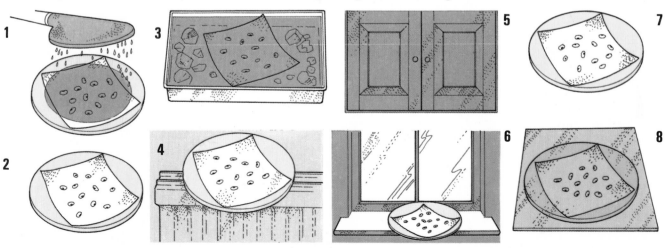

Leaf skeleton

Leaves and stems are given their shape by the woody vessels which conduct water around the plant. These vessels work in a similar way to the human system of veins and arteries. If you hold up a leaf to the light, you can observe its woody skeleton. But if you want to study the system of leaf veins closely, you can try this experiment to make a leaf skeleton.

Procedure

1. Choose a variety of fallen **leaves** for this project. Try looking in your backyard or in a local park or woods. You might want to take a tree guidebook with you so that you can identify the leaves as you find them.

2. Fill a large, old **saucepan** about two-thirds full of water. Add a spoonful of **washing soda**. Then bring the water to a boil. Add a few leaves and boil for about one hour. Check the pan frequently to make sure it does not boil dry. Boil any additional leaves in the same way.

3. In a **plastic tub**, make a solution of **household bleach** and water. Use about one part bleach to six parts water. Wear **rubber gloves** when using bleach, and make sure you do not spill any bleach or solution on your clothes or skin.

4. Using a **slotted spoon**, carefully lower the boiled leaves into the bleach solution. Leave them overnight. In the morning, everything except the skeleton of leaf veins will have floated away.

5. Remove the leaves with a slotted spoon and place them on **paper towels** or white paper to dry. Discard the bleach solution carefully. When your skeletons are completely dry, you can mount them if you wish on **cardboard**.

You will need—

leaves
saucepan
washing soda
plastic tub
household bleach
rubber gloves
slotted spoon
paper towels
cardboard

Take care!

Make sure to protect your clothes and work area when using bleach. Mop up any spills immediately, and wash your skin thoroughly if the bleach solution splashes onto it.

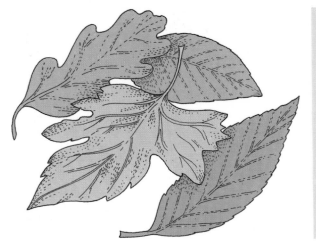

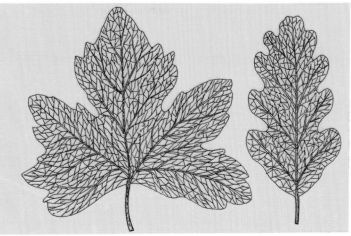

Mold garden

You will need—

2 glass jars with lids
slice of bread
bruised apple

Molds are a group of simple organisms belonging to the fungi family. Because molds cannot make their own food, they live as parasites on other plants or animals. There are several types of mold, some of them useful to man. Molds are used in making some types of fertilizer. Certain cheeses, like blue cheese, depend on mold as a flavoring and ripening agent. The anti-bacterial drug penicillin is derived from mold. Try this experiment and grow your own mold garden.

Procedure
1. You will need two clean, dry **glass jars** with lids. Put a **slice of bread** (white sandwich loaf works well) on a plate. Expose it to the air for an hour or so. Mold spores will fall upon the exposed bread. Now sprinkle the bread lightly with water and place it in one of the jars.
2. Find an **apple** that has been bruised. If you cannot find a bruised apple, you could use another kind of fruit. Put the bruised fruit into the other jar.
3. Put the lids on both jars and place them in a warm, dark place for a week. At the end of the week, remove the jars. The bread will be covered with a cotton-like growth of white stalks with tiny black balls on the ends. These are the spore cases. The mold and bacteria working on the fruit in the second jar will have rotted it. After examining the mold, discard the fruit and the slice of bread and wash the jars thoroughly.

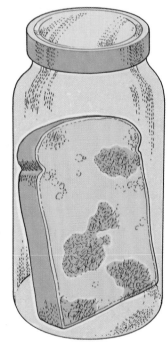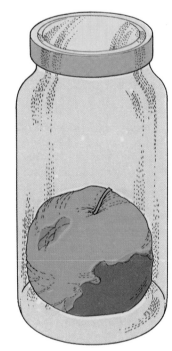

MORE DIFFICULT PROJECTS

The more difficult projects and experiments found in the following pages will help you to explore the relationships plants and animals have with each other and with their surroundings. Learn how to propagate and clone plants, and how to grow plants without soil. You can also construct a formicarium to study a community of ants, and recreate an animal's natural habitat in a vivarium. Make a plankton net, then observe microscopic pond life; or you can study soil erosion and test ways to control it.

Plants without soil -¤-

You will need—

aquarium
wire mesh
2 teaspoons calcium
   nitrate
1¼ teaspoons Epsom
   salts
½ teaspoon potassium
   acid phosphate
¼ teaspoon ammonium
   sulfate
distilled water
⅛ teaspoon boric acid
⅛ teaspoon
   manganese sulfate
⅛ teaspoon zinc sulfate
⅛ teaspoon ferrous
   sulfate
sphagnum moss
corn and bean seeds

Hydroponics is the science of growing plants without soil. Scientists discovered this technique in the mid-1800s when trying to find a way to study the root development and nutritional needs of plants. They knew that soil contains several essential growth nutrients, like nitrogen, potassium, and phosphorus. The scientists decided to suspend seeds in a solution of these nutrients mixed with water. They found that the seeds grew as well as seeds grown in soil.

There are two main types of hydroponics: water culture and aggregate culture. In water culture, plants or seeds are suspended on a bed over a tank of nutrient solution. The roots grow down into the solution, and absorb the nutrients essential for growth. In aggregate culture, the plants are anchored in a coarse material like gravel or sand. The nutrient solution is constantly circulated throughout the anchoring material.

Hydroponics is not only useful for growing off-season plants, it is also helpful in determining the specific nutritional needs of plants. Laboratory technicians can add more or less of certain nutrients to the growth solution to find the best ratio for successful growth. Try experimenting with hydroponics in this project.

Procedure

1. You will need an **aquarium** for this project. Ask an adult to help you cut a piece of **wire mesh** to the same width as the aquarium, but to a length several inches longer than the inside dimensions of the tank. Bend the ends of the wire mesh and put it inside the aquarium as shown so that it forms a "table." The table should be only a few inches above the floor of the aquarium.

2. Make solution A: Dissolve 2 teaspoons of **calcium nitrate**, 1¼ teaspoons of **Epsom salts**, ½ teaspoon of **potassium acid phosphate**, and ¼ teaspoon of **ammonium sulfate** into one cup of water. Add this mixture to 2½ gallons of **distilled water**.

3. To make solution B, dissolve ⅛ teaspoon of each of these three materials in a cup of water: **boric acid**, **manganese sulfate**, and **zinc sulfate**.

4. Solution C is made by dissolving ⅛ teaspoon of **ferrous sulfate** into a cup of water. Now add 1 teaspoon of solution B and 3 tablespoons of solution C to solution A.

5. Pour the mixture you have prepared into the tank up to the level of the wire mesh table. Then sprinkle a layer of **sphagnum moss** (peat moss) over the wire table. This moss will help to anchor the seeds.

6. Scatter the **corn and bean seeds** randomly over the top of the moss. Over the next few days, the seeds will germinate and grow roots reaching down to the solution. Continue to refill the aquarium with fresh solution during the growing period to maintain its level. You might want to try this experiment with other plants, such as tomatoes, which are often grown hydroponically off-season.

Take care!

Be careful when using and mixing the chemicals, and store them in a safe place, away from young children and pets. Because a filled aquarium is so heavy, it is best to put it in its permanent position before adding the growth solution.

Ant house ⊹

You will need–

wooden seed tray
heavy plastic
piece of wood
plaster of Paris
old plastic bowl
spoon
soil
household cement
2 pieces of glass or
   plastic glass
ants
honey
black cardboard

Ants are insects that live in highly-organized communities called colonies. There are around 10,000 species of ants, ranging in size from about 1/25 of an inch long to more than one inch long. Ants are found in all types of environments, except those with extremely cold climates. You can observe your own colony of ants by making this formicarium.

An ant colony can have anywhere from a dozen to a million members, but all colonies have one or more queens. The main duty of the queen ant or ants is to lay eggs. Queen ants are usually much larger than other ants. The queen has her own chamber in the nest, or home, which she rarely leaves. During her lifetime, the queen ant may lay thousands of eggs.

Most other members of the ant colony are called workers. Workers have several important tasks: they build and maintain the nest, find food for the queen and her young, watch over the young ants, and defend the nest from enemies. Some species of ants have larger workers called soldiers.

Male ants visit the nest during mating season, but do not usually live there. After male ants fertilize the eggs, they leave the nest, often wandering off to die.

This project will show you how to build a formicarium, or ant house, so that you can study and observe these fascinating creatures. Remember to feed the ants often with honey, water, or tiny pieces of fruit. You should also keep the formicarium covered.

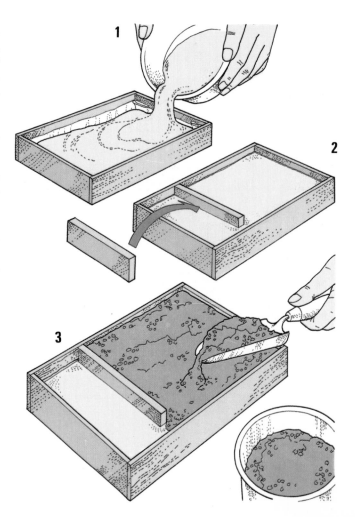

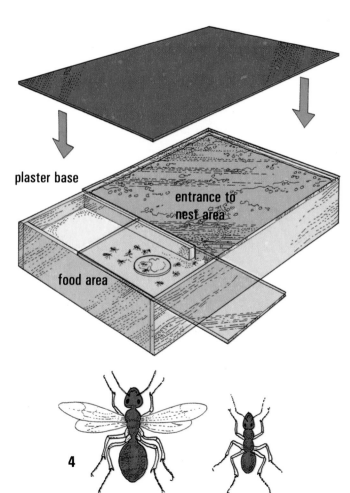

plaster base

entrance to nest area

food area

4

Procedure

1. Buy a **wooden seed tray** about 16 inches by 12 inches from a garden center. Line the bottom and sides of the tray with a sheet of **heavy plastic**. Then ask an adult to cut a **piece of wood** 3 inches deep and 1¼ inches shorter than the width of the seed tray.

2. Mix up some **plaster of Paris** and water in an old **plastic bowl** with an old **spoon**, following the directions on the package. Pour the mixture into the tray to within 1¼ inches from the top.

3. Lay the wood in the wet plaster about 4 inches from one end, so the top is level with the rim of the tray as shown. Let the plaster dry thoroughly.

4. You will be using the smaller part of the tray as the feeding area and the entrance, and the larger part will serve as the nest. Fill the larger part with fine **soil**. Using **household cement**, fix a **glass** or plastic glass cover over it. Cover the smaller area with a piece of glass, but do not cement it. You will need access to the smaller area so that you can feed the ants.

5. Look under stones and fallen trees in your backyard or a nearby park for **ants**. You will need a queen ant—she is the biggest ant, and may have wings. Put the ants, some **honey**, and a few drops of water into the smaller area and cover with the glass. Keep a sheet of **black cardboard** over the nest unless you are observing it. Remember to give water as well as food to the ants.

Take care!

Wipe up any splashes of plaster before they set. Once they are hard, they will be difficult to remove. You should also be careful when handling the edges of glass. Cover them with masking tape if they are sharp.

Ecology notebook

notebook and pencil
magnifying glass
white paper
clean jars
binoculars and
   camera, if wished

You might not think that your backyard is rich in plant and animal life, with many different habitats, or places for plants and animals to live. But this project will help you to take a closer look at your own habitat. When you observe and record all the small plants and creatures you find, you might be astonished by how much life surrounds you.

Ecology is the branch of biology concerned with everything about plants and animals, especially the relationships they have with each other and with their surroundings, or environment. Ecologists also study how changes in the environment affect the plants and animals living within it.

A group of plants and animals existing together in a particular environment is called an ecosystem. The ecosystem can be as small as a pond or as large as a tropical rainforest. Members of the ecosystem depend on each other in many ways. In a pond, for example, water plants provide food and oxygen for the animals that live in the pond. The plants, in turn, depend on wastes from the animals to keep them alive. A balance between the plants and animals of an ecosystem is essential for life; if the water in the pond becomes polluted and the plants die off, the animals will be unable to find food and they, too, will die.

In this project, you will be treating your backyard as an ecosystem. If you do not have a yard, you could study a neighbor's yard or a local park. You will need several items to help you with your study: a **notebook** and **pencil** to record your findings, a small **magnifying glass**, a long roll of **white paper** to collect insect specimens shaken out of branches, and some **clean jars** to keep any specimens you want to have a closer look at. If you own or can borrow a pair of **binoculars**, you might want to use them to examine distant objects. You may also want to have a **camera** handy.

An unusual way to begin is to choose one object to observe. It might be a tree, a pile of raked leaves, or a flower bed. Look carefully at the object you have chosen, taking notes if you like. Then take one step backward. You should now be able to observe the object and part of its surroundings. Continue to observe and step backward. In this way, you should slowly become aware of the relationships between the living things.

As you observe the ecosystem, keep notes on any creatures you find and where you find them. You may want to add a sketch of the creature. Look closely at holes in fences or walls, under branches or rotting wood, and in any pools of water.

white paper

notebook

pencil

magnifying glass

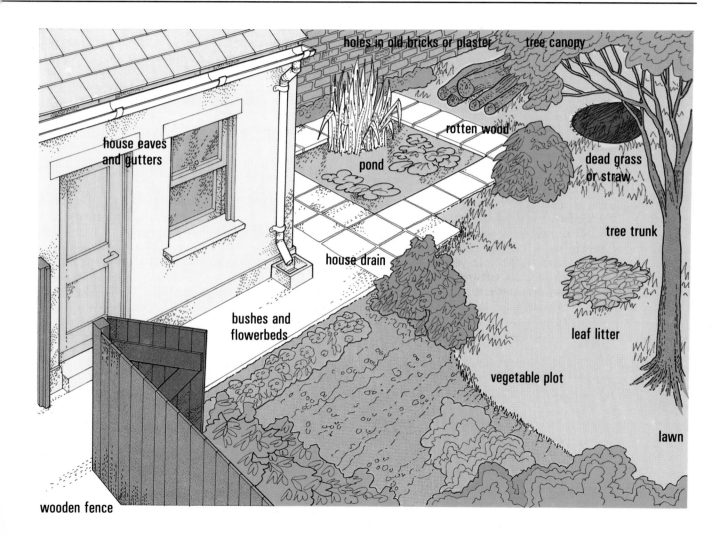

holes in old bricks or plaster

tree canopy

rotten wood

house eaves
and gutters

dead grass
or straw

pond

tree trunk

house drain

leaf litter

bushes and
flowerbeds

vegetable plot

lawn

wooden fence

Vivarium ⎓

You will need—

aquarium tank
acrylic sheet
animal (see chart)
soil (see chart)
old bowl
jar lids
stones
twigs or branches
plants (see chart)

You can raise small animals in their natural habitats by making this vivarium.

Procedure

1. An **aquarium tank** makes a good vivarium. (If you do not have an aquarium tank, you could ask an adult to build a three-sided softwood box instead. Fit a sheet of glass for the fourth side of the box, and construct a lid following the directions in step 2. Line the bottom with a piece of plastic turned up against the sides.)

2. Make a lid for the tank. You will need to buy a **sheet of acrylic** from a specialist supplier. Take the dimensions of the tank to the supplier, and ask to have it cut at the store. Then ask an adult to make several air holes in the acrylic sheet, using a suitable drill bit. If there is no acrylic sheet supplier in your area, you could ask an adult to construct a softwood frame to fit the top of the tank. Stretch a piece of wire mesh over the frame and fix it into place with staple pins.

3. When your vivarium is complete, choose an **animal**. Your choice of animal will determine what kinds of soil, plants, and other things you will need. Read some books from the library or ask a sales assistant at a pet shop what conditions and food an animal likes best before you decide to raise one.

4. Use the chart below to choose a **soil**. Put a layer of soil about an inch deep in the bottom of the vivarium. You can make a pond by sinking an **old bowl** or even a few **jar lids** into the soil, then filling with water. Slope the soil away from the pond and surround it with **stones**. Add a few **twigs or branches** for climbing. Put **plants** directly into the soil, or grow them in pots and then sink these into the soil.

5. Remember to feed your animal regularly. In addition to food from the pet store, you can catch your own. Find worms under stones or logs in your backyard or catch insects with a butterfly net. Always put dead food in a bowl, and make sure the pond has fresh water.

	Soil	Plants	Conditions	Food
Frogs and toads 	Moist soil mixed with peat.	Swiss cheese plant and pond weeds.	Small pond with rock in it for sitting on. Keep the vivarium in a shady place at all times.	All insects; worms and mealwoms. Feed once or twice a week.
 **Lizards**	Dry soil mixed with gravel and sand.	Sweetheart plant and ivy. Dry bracken or moss to scratch dead skin against.	Rocks; sticks or branches. Put the vivarium in a warm spot for a few hours each day.	Live insects. Feed about twice a week.

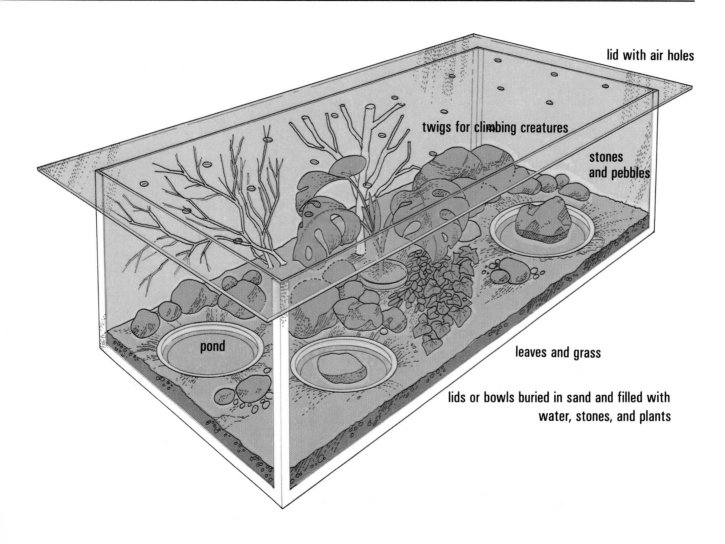

lid with air holes

twigs for climbing creatures

stones
and pebbles

pond

leaves and grass

lids or bowls buried in sand and filled with
water, stones, and plants

Take care!

Aquarium tanks are
heavy – it is best to put
the tank in its permanent
position before adding
soil, plants, and animals.

Plankton fishing ⊡

You will need—

small, screw-top bottle
tape measure
old scissors
No. 20 mesh size silk or
  synthetic fiber net
brass or galvanized
  iron ring, 8 inch
  circumference
cotton thread and
  needle
nylon cord
small metal ring
heavy twine
old fishing rod or broom
  handle
small lead fishing
  weights

Plankton is a general name for the plant and animal life found on, or just below, the surface of a body of water. Plankton can be found both in oceans and in freshwater lakes. They are too small or weak to swim, so they are carried from place to place by currents.

Plankton is made up of a variety of organisms. The plantlike group of plankton is called phytoplankton. Phytoplankton is made up of tiny, one-celled plants too small to be seen without a microscope. Blue-green alga and diatom are two of the numerous types of organism found in this group. Animal plankton is called zooplankton. Zooplankton contains not only eggs and larvae of water creatures, like fish and squid, but also all animals that live their complete life cycles in a floating state. Jellyfish and crustaceans are two common types of zooplankton.

Plankton is a crucial part of the ocean and freshwater food chains. Larger animals, like fish, feed on plankton; humans, in turn, eat fish. Plankton is also linked with the creation of natural gas. Scientists speculate that millions of years ago, plankton died and sank to the ocean floors. Over time, layers of sand and mud covered and compressed the plankton, changing the chemical compound found in the plankton into natural gas and oil. Scientists hope to use plankton in the future as an inexpensive, widely available food source.

In this project, you can fish for these important organisms by making a plankton net. You can use your net from the shore of a pond or lake or in the still part of a creek. If you attach small lead weights to the net, you can fish from a boat. You can then examine and identify your "catch" by following the guidelines found on pages 32–3.

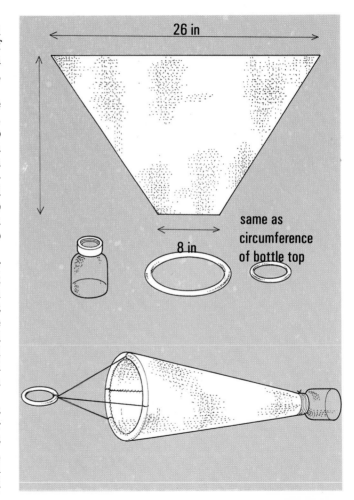

26 in

8 in

same as circumference of bottle top

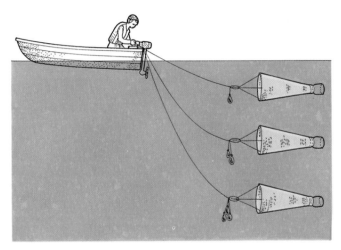

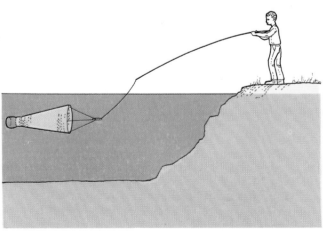

Procedure

1. You will need a **small, screw-top bottle**. Using a **tape measure**, measure around the outside of the cap to find its circumference. Then, using **old scissors**, cut away the top of the cap carefully.

2. Buy a length of **silk or synthetic fiber net**, number 20 mesh size. Cut the net to the shape and dimensions shown, with a 26-inch top tapering down to the bottom, which should be the same measurement as the circumference of the bottle cap.

3. Now sew the top of the net over the **large metal ring**, using **cotton thread**. Overstitching is the best method to use. When you have finished sewing the net to the ring, sew the side seam firmly all the way to the bottom of the net.

4. Now make the pulling ring. Cut three lengths of thin **nylon cord**, each 12 inches long. Attach one end of each piece of cord in turn to the **small metal ring**, then attach the other ends to the large brass ring as shown. Make sure the knots are secure.

5. To attach the net to the collecting bottle, twist off its cap. Using **heavy twine**, bind the cap into the net, then screw the cap back onto the bottle.

6. To use your net from the shore, you will need to attach it to a long pole. You could use an **old fishing rod** or **broom handle**. Tie a length of strong nylon cord to the small metal pulling ring and attach the other end very firmly to the pole. Make sure the knots are very secure before using the net. Choose a safe place to stand on the edge of the pond. Make slow, gentle sweeps just below the surface of the pond for the best results. You could also "fish" from a boat as shown. Add small **lead weights** to fish deeper.

Take care!

Stand well away from the edge of the pond when plankton fishing. Only experienced boaters should try plankton fishing from a boat.

Pond life

You will need—

water sample
2 petri dishes or shallow
  glass bowls
magnifying glass
tweezers
formalin
microscope slides
cover glasses
medicine dropper
microscope
notebook and pencil

In this project, you can investigate the microscopic life of a pond. You will need a microscope that can magnify by at least 400×. If you do not have a microscope of your own, ask your teacher if you can use one in your school science lab to examine your slides.

Procedure
1. You will need a **water sample** from a pond for this experiment. If you have made the plankton fishing net on pages 30–1, you can use a sample of water from your collecting jar. If you have not made the plankton net, you will need one or two clean glass jars to serve as collecting bottles. Stand near the edge of a pond or a still part of a creek. Gently sweep the open jar just under the surface of the water, scooping up any plant matter floating on the surface, and replace the lid.
2. Pour some of the water into a **petri dish** or a **shallow glass bowl**. Use a **magnifying glass** to examine the sample. If you see a moving object, pluck it from the water carefully with a pair of **tweezers**. Put it in an empty petri dish or glass bowl and put one or two drops of **formalin** on the object. (Formalin is a solution of formaldehyde which kills and preserves organisms.)
3. Now carefully lift the object with the tweezers onto a **microscope slide**. Then use the tweezers to cover the object with a **cover glass**.
4. Make some additional slides to study. You can repeat steps 2 and 3 with any other living objects you find. You can also use a **medicine dropper** to put a few drops of pond water in the center of another slide. Cover the water with a cover glass. Prepare a few more slides in this way. Lift out a small sample of any plant matter in your collecting jar, put it on a slide, and add a cover glass.
5. Now observe your slides with the **microscope**. Vary the magnification and move the slide around so that you can see all of it. Can you identify any of the objects you have found? Use the drawings on the right to help you. You might want to keep your **notebook** and **pencil** beside you so that you can make a sketch of the objects you have found.

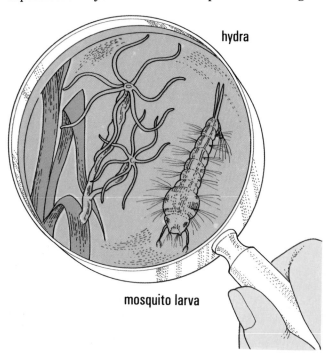

hydra

mosquito larva

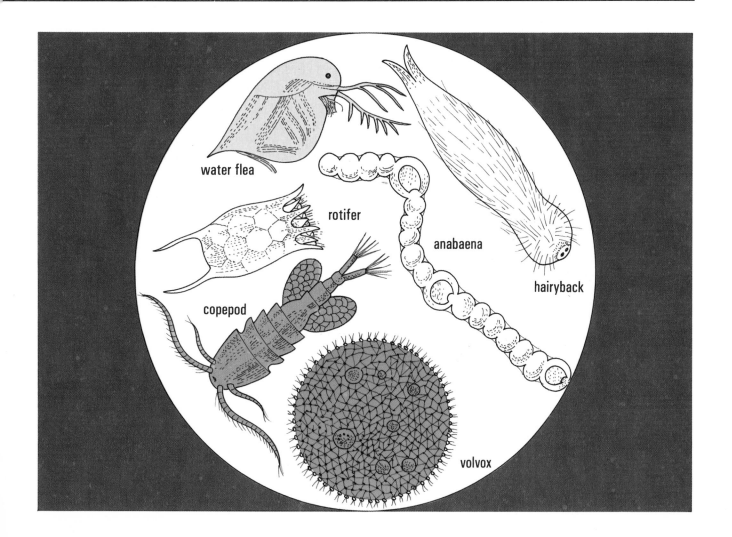

water flea

rotifer

anabaena

hairyback

copepod

volvox

Soil erosion

You will need—

3 aluminum foil cake
  pans
scissors
rubber tubing
cellophane tape
clay
soil
sand
topsoil
scrap wood
3 glass or plastic bowls
cereal grain seed
sprinkling can

Erosion is the process by which earth materials such as rock and soil are broken loose from the earth's surface and carried away. Erosion is usually a slow and gradual process. Many North American mounain ranges, for example, were created by thousands of years of glacial erosion. The spectacular contours of the Grand Canyon were carved out by millions of years of erosion from the Colorado River.

The first step in the process of erosion is called weathering. Weathering is the breaking down of earth materials into smaller pieces. Various environmental factors, like ice formation, heat from the sun, and movement of air and water, all contribute to the process of weathering.

Once materials have been loosened by weathering, they are transported to new locations by erosion. Wind and running water are the two main agents of erosion. Heavy rains can wash soil particles downhill, for example, and strong winds can lift and carry soil and rock particles over great distances.

Not all erosion is a result of environmental processes. Intensive farming and mining speed up the process of erosion and can have quite harmful effects. When land is cleared for cultivation, for example, trees and other plants that help to shield the land from erosion by wind and rain are removed. As a result, the valuable topsoil is put at risk. Farmers use several methods to help limit the erosion of topsoil. They may plant cover crops like alfalfa or grass on valuable land, or employ tillage techniques which allow wastes from old crops to remain on the soil. This experiment will show you the effects of soil erosion, and one of the most common methods of reducing it.

Procedure

1. You will need three large **aluminum foil cake pans**. Cut a small hole near the top rim on one side of each pan with **scissors**. Then cut three pieces of **rubber tubing**, each about nine inches long. **Tape** a piece of tubing into each hole. Make the holes a little larger, if necessary.

2. Next, fill each cake pan with layers of **clay**, **soil**, and **sand**. Add a top layer of rich **topsoil** to each pan.

3. Find a block of **scrap wood**. Rest one end of each of

1

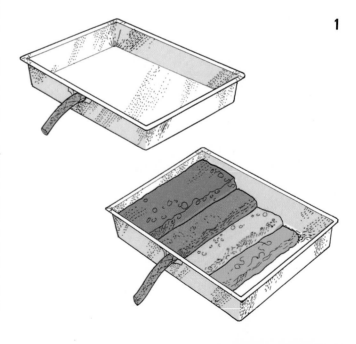

the three pans on the block of wood to elevate it to a 30° angle, with the hose pointing downward. Put an old **glass or plastic bowl** below each pan. Direct the hoses into the bowls to collect excess water.

4. Now plant your crops. In the first pan, make horizontal rows across the topsoil and plant a **cereal grain** such as wheat, oats, or barley.

5. In the second pan, make vertical rows in the topsoil and plant the same cereal grain. Do not plant anything in the third pan.

6. Using a **sprinkling can** to simulate rain, water the three pans regularly, using the same amount of water over each pan. Observe carefully over the next few days. What is happening to the topsoil in each pan?

7. The first pan is a simulation of contour farming. In this method the farmer sows the seeds around a hill. The second pan shows the seeds sown up and down the hill. You should find that the second method prevents more soil erosion than the unplanted third pan, but neither is more efficient than the first pan.

2

3

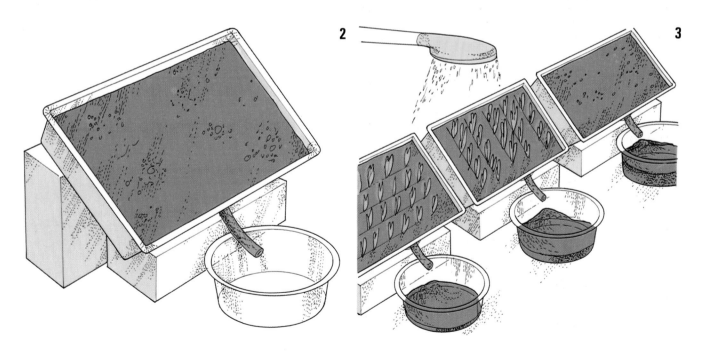

Propagation and cloning

3 plants: African violet,
  spider plant, and
  Impatiens
3 small flowerpots
cutting board
sharp knife
rooting powder
seed and cutting soil
shallow dish
gravel
plastic bag
rubber band
glass custard cup
cardboard
scissors

New plants grown from the cells of a parent plant are genetically identical, and are called clones. In this project, you will be propagating and cloning plants by three different methods.

Hereditary units called genes are found deep inside the chromosomes of plants. These genes contain "instructions" about the growth of the plant. Such factors as a flower's color and size are contained within these genetic instructions.

If you want to create a new plant from the cells of a parent plant, you can do so by leaf cutting, offshoots, and stem cutting. In leaf cutting, a leaf from the parent plant is placed in water to develop roots. In the offshoot method, a plantlet is separated from the parent and put in soil to develop roots. A portion of a parent plant's stem grows roots in water in the stem cutting method. Try all three methods to propagate some common houseplants.

Leaf cutting

Procedure

1. To clone plants by leaf cutting, you will need three healthy, medium-sized leaves from an **African violet**. On a **cutting board** with a **sharp knife**, trim the ends to a length of about 3 inches. Dip the ends in **rooting powder** (available in garden centers) and plant them in a pot of **seed and cutting soil**. Put the pot in a **shallow dish** filled with **gravel** to provide good drainage. Water the pot from below, then cover it with a **plastic bag** secured with a **rubber band** as shown.
2. After about three days, remove the plastic bag. Water your new plant from below as needed.

Offshoots

Procedure

1. To clone plants by the offshoot method, you will need to find a **spider plant** that has several plantlets on it. These plantlets look just like miniature spider plants.
2. Break off a plantlet from the end of a healthy spider plant as shown. Pot it immediately in suitable soil and water the new plant thoroughly.

Stem cutting

Procedure

1. You will need a healthy **Impatiens plant**, or a touch-me-not. Take a stem cutting with a few leaves from the plant.
2. To root the plant, find a small **glass custard cup** or shallow bowl. Cut a circle of **cardboard** to cover it. Using **scissors**, carefully cut a hole in the middle of the cardboard. If you are rooting two cuttings, cut two holes. Put the cuttings through the holes in the cardboard as shown. When the cuttings have grown roots, pot them in suitable soil and water the new plants thoroughly.

leaf cutting

stem cutting

offshoot

Live yeast

You will need—

jar
5 teaspoons sugar
spoon
bottle
1 teaspoon yeast
balloon
string
glass jar
limewater (see
   instructions in text)

Yeast is a tiny, living fungus that gives off carbon dioxide gas as a by-product of its reproduction. Yeast is found almost everywhere, even in the air. Yeast is added to bread dough before baking because the carbon dioxide gas makes it rise. It is also an essential ingredient in the production of wine and other alcoholic beverages, and is sometimes used as a dietary supplement because it is so rich in protein.

The valuable properties of yeast were discovered by accident. Sometime around 2600 B.C., an Egyptian baker may have added some old bread dough that had

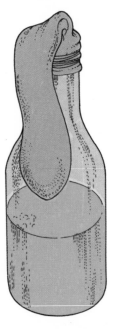

been left uncovered to some new bread dough. The yeast organisms that had fallen on the old dough while it was exposed to the air served as a leaven, or raising agent, for the new dough. Although the recipe was passed down for thousands of years, no one really understood how the process worked.

In 1876, however, the brilliant French scientist Louis Pasteur explained that yeasts were living cells. He speculated that yeasts were crucial in baking and brewing. By the late 1800s, yeast became commercially available.

Yeasts reproduce in two ways: fission and budding. In fission, the yeast cells split in two. In the budding process, the cell wall swells and develops a small growth called a bud. This bud splits off to become a new cell.

Yeasts are not able to make their own food; they can, however, break down the food they find. Yeasts make fermenting chemicals called enzymes to break down sugars. When making bread, for example, yeast is mixed with sugar and water. The yeast feeds on the sugar and begins to grow. The growth process continues when flour and salt are added, and carbon dioxide gas released as a result forms little air pockets in the dough which make it light and well-risen.

Try this experiment to see how sugar and yeast react. You will need to make limewater for this experiment: stir a teaspoon of garden lime into a jar of water from the faucet. Be sure to wash your hands after using lime.

Procedure

1. You will need an old, clean **jar**. Fill it halfway with warm water from the faucet. Add five teaspoons of

sugar. Stir with a **spoon** until the sugar is completely dissolved.

2. Pour the sugar solution into a clean **bottle** and wash out the empty jar.

3. Mix one teaspoon of **yeast** and two teaspoons of water in the jar. Carefully pour the yeast mixture into the sugar solution in the bottle.

4. Attach a **balloon** tightly to the neck of the bottle. Use a piece of **string** and tie it several times around the neck of the bottle so that the balloon stays put. Now put the bottle in a warm place.

5. Now fill a wide-mouthed, empty **glass jar** with **limewater.** Set it aside.

6. Check the bottle of yeast and sugar solution. The solution will begin to bubble, and slowly the balloon will be inflated by gas.

7. Carefully pinch the neck of the balloon so that the gas does not escape and remove it from the bottle. Put the end of the balloon under the surface of the jar of limewater, still pinching it together tightly. Now release the gas slowly. The carbon dioxide in the balloon will turn the limewater a milky color.

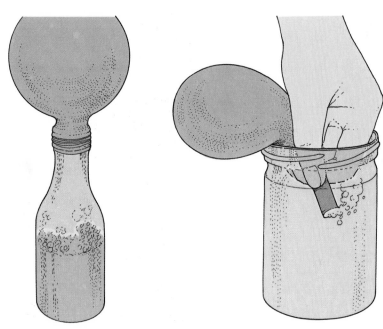

SAFETY FIRST!

The safe and simple projects and experiments in this book cover many fields of science and technology, and have been designed to demonstrate and explain important scientific principles in an interesting and straightforward way. Good scientists take care to protect themselves and other people, so always follow these rules for perfect safety.

*FIRE Take care when using matches or candles, and keep a pail of water nearby in case of accidents.

*MAIN LINE ELECTRICITY Use low-power batteries as directed in this book. Do not use the main line—it can kill.

*CHEMICALS Use with care, label clearly, and store out of reach of young children and animals.

*SHARP EDGES Where possible, file edges smooth, and always protect your hands with thick gloves.

And remember . . . before you begin, always get permission from an adult, and if in doubt, ask for help!

SAFETY

The chemicals used in the projects can all be handled safely. Most are common household substances such as salt, baking powder, vinegar, etc.

When a project calls for an electricity supply, there is no danger of electric shock because a low-voltage battery is used.

A few projects involve the use of a flame or heat from a stove. In such cases, younger experimenters should be supervised by an adult, but the procedure is as safe as cooking.

SUPERVISION

The projects have been graded according to the need for adult supervision. Where a project is marked with an ⊕, it means that, for complete safety, an adult should assist the young experimenter with some aspects of the project. In many cases, the adult's assistance will be limited to helping with some parts of the project, such as using a hammer and nails, and then letting the experimenter continue the project with only background supervision. Similarly, it may be necessary for an adult to handle matches or candles.

In other cases, the adult can prepare the materials which are needed for the experiment.

For example, if the project includes accurate cutting out with a sharp knife, the experimenter need not handle the knife if the adult does the cutting out beforehand.

It is a good idea for an adult to be present when the project involves breakable objects like glass jars. A little guidance will minimize the risk of breakages.

SHARP EDGES

Wherever it is possible, the materials chosen for the projects are the safest ones that can be used. Sometimes, there is a choice of materials. For instance, the risk of sharp edges is reduced if you use plastic glass, but if you do use conventional glass, the chance of getting cut will be minimized if you are careful. First, protect your hands with gloves and use a small file or some sandpaper to remove any sharp edges. Handle the glass carefully and never put too much strain on it.

Similar precautions should be taken if the project involves cutting metal. Again, wear gloves and file off any sharp points. For extra safety, cover the cut edges with thick cellophane tape. If the project uses an empty tin can, try to find a can with a push-fit lid. This means you do not need to use a can opener, which will leave a sharp edge.

CHEMICALS

The chemicals used in the projects are all harmless, but they should still be treated with care. Keep each chemical in a labeled jar, and make sure that the jars are stored out of reach of inquisitive small children. Do not experiment with chemicals anywhere near food. Cover the worktable with old newspaper; it will catch any spilt chemicals and can be thrown away later. After the experiment, wash thoroughly the jars or dishes that have been used and pour the old chemicals down the sink, flushing them away with lots of water. Finally, wash your hands thoroughly to remove any traces of chemicals on the skin.

FIRE

You should take extra care with those projects which involve matches or candles. Organize the worktable so that there are no scraps of paper lying around and make sure that you are not wearing loose clothing, such as a tie or scarf, which might accidentally catch fire. Check that you have all the materials needed for the experiment before you begin and arrange them on the worktable so that you do not need to reach over the candle. Always keep a pail of water close at hand just in case there is an accident.

PROCEDURE

Before starting work on a project, it is important to read the instructions through to the end and to form a clear idea of what has to be done, and in what order. Materials and tools needed are listed in the margin and are spelled out in **bold type** when they are first mentioned. Make sure that everything is at hand when it is needed. Many of the projects or experiments can be carried out more smoothly if a little preparatory work, like weighing or cutting out, is done beforehand.

SCIENCE AND THE FUTURE

There are more and more opportunities for scientists in the modern world. Every year, new scientific discoveries help to change the world we live in. Most aspects of our life, including transport, entertainment, medicine, and industry are changing rapidly because of the new inventions and discoveries that scientists are making. When you work on the projects in this book, you will learn many of the basic scientific principles which have helped important scientists to make their contribution to our world. Maybe one day, if you decide to become a scientist, you will join the great men and women of science who will create the world of the future.

WORDS YOU NEED TO KNOW

In this book, you may find some words that you have not seen before. These four pages explain as simply as possible what these words mean and will help you to understand exactly how to do the projects or experiments. Some words are special descriptions invented by scientists, and so are often very complicated to explain — in fact, whole books have been written about them! Of course, there is not enough space in this book to include these very long explanations but if you want to read more, ask your teacher or librarian to help you find a book.

Absorb
To swallow up or take in

Antennae
Pair of movable sense organs attached to the head of an insect; feelers

Aphid
A plant louse

Atmosphere
The air in any given place; the gases around Earth

Bud
Small swelling or projection

Burrow
To dig a hole or tunnel

Carbon dioxide
Colorless, odorless gas

Carnivore
Flesh-eating animal

Cell
Most basic element of living creatures or structures

Chromosome
Threadlike chain of cells in the body that passes on a parent's features to a child

Chrysalis
The case enveloping an insect between larva and adult stages; pupa

Clone
A group of plants directly descended from a single individual

Compress
To condense or press together

Conduct
To convey or transmit

Contract
To grow smaller

Current
Flow or movement of water or electricty

Ecology
Branch of biology dealing with living things and their environment

Ecosystem
Any community of animals, plants, and bacteria

Environment
The conditions and influences surrounding and affecting a group of organisms

Enzyme
An organic substance that causes a change in other substances

Erosion
In geology, the wearing away of the earth's surface

Ferment
To break down complex molecules in organic substances

Fertilizer
A material put in soil to improve the quality of plants grown in it

Fission
In biology, a form of reproduction in which the parent organism splits into two or more parts

Formaldehyde
A strong, colorless gas, used as a preservative

Formicarium
The nest of a community of ants

Fungus
A plant with no green color, for example, mushroom and mold

Gas
Air or vapor; a form of a substance which is neither liquid nor solid

Gene
Element contained in reproductive cells which carries hereditary information

Germinate
To sprout, shoot, or bud

Glacial
Of a large mass of moving snow and ice

Habitat
Home or dwelling of an animal or plant

Hydroponics
The science of growing plants in nutrient solutions instead of in soil

Infest
To attack or disturb

Infrared
Invisible rays just beyond the visible spectrum

Larva
An insect in the earliest stage of development after it has hatched

Leaven
A substance that creates fermentation

Life cycle
The series of changes in form an organism undergoes

Lime
A white substance used to treat soil

Mold
Furry growth on the surface of organic matter

Molt
To shed layers of skin during growth

Nest
Home for a living creature

Nutrient
Substance that provides nourishment

Organism
Living plant or animal

Parasite
A plant or animal that lives on or inside another

Peat
A moisture-absorbing plant matter

Pesticide
Chemical used to kill insects or weeds

Petri dish
Shallow, round dish

Propagate
To cause reproduction

Pupa
An insect in the stage of life between larval and adult

Ray
The path of a beam of light or energy

Root
Part of a plant which draws and stores water and food from the soil, and holds it in place

Sapling
A young tree

Seed coat
Outside covering of a seed

Segmented
Divided into sections

Solution
Homogenous mixture of something with water

Species
A single, distinct kind of plant or animal

Specimen
A sample or example

Sphagnum moss
Pale gray aquatic plant, used to make fertilizer

Spinneret
Tiny organ with which caterpillars spin threads

Stage
A growth period

Subsoil
Earth below the surface soil

Tillage
To plow and prepare land for growing crops

Topsoil
Rich, dark surface earth

Vivarium
An enclosed place for raising plants or animals in conditions similar to their natural habitats

INDEX